MOTORING
in the 'Twenties & 'Thirties

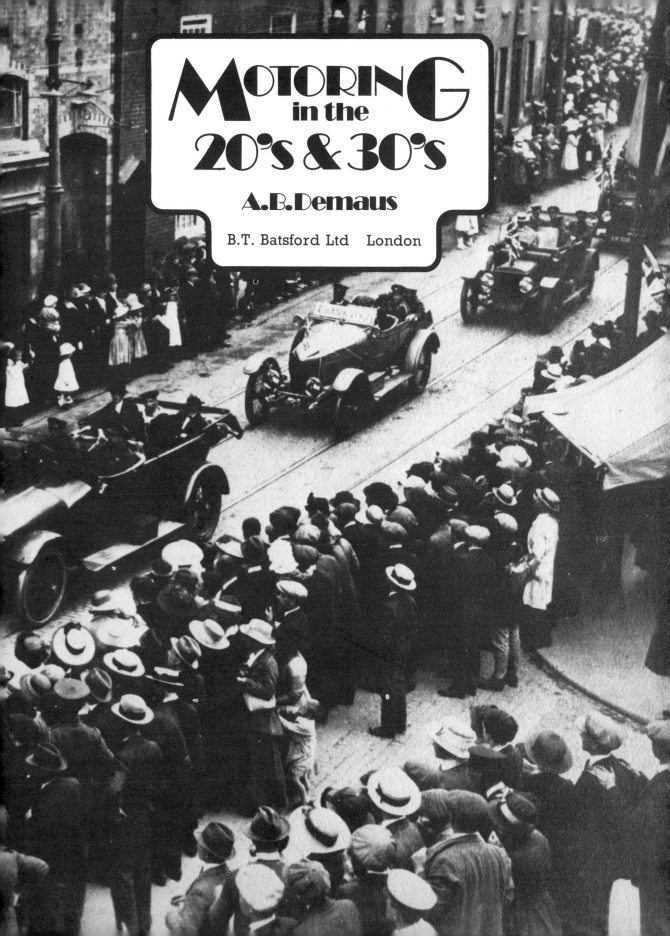

Motoring
in the
20's & 30's

A.B.Demaus

B.T. Batsford Ltd   London

Frontispiece The dawn of a new era. A formal
Armistice Parade passes through the streets of
Worcester in 1918 with a Singer, a Crossley, a
Vauxhall 'Prince Henry' and a Daimler leading the
procession. The cars all date from the pre-war
period but the coming of peace did not restore the
old order which had gone for ever. Although this
Parade marked the end of 'the war to end wars' the
majority of those present would be embroiled in war
again in the space of a short twenty-one years

ISBN 0 7134 1538 X

Filmset in 'Monophoto' Rockwell by
Service Filmsetting Ltd, Manchester

Printed in Great Britain by
The Anchor Press Ltd, Tiptree, Essex

for the Publishers
B.T. Batsford Ltd, 4 Fitzhardinge Street
London W1H 0AH

Contents

Acknowledgment

The author owes a real debt of gratitude to innumerable people who have endured, put up with, or even in any way encouraged his obsessive love of motor cars since the age of four or thereabouts, and in a narrower field but with no less genuine gratitude to the many who have most kindly allowed him access to private photographs of motoring topics. Because the majority of the photographs have come from private sources it has not always been possible to identify the photographer or the original source with any certainty, and if someone's copyright has thus been inadvertently infringed, the author craves forgiveness and indulgence.

The author gratefully acknowledges the following sources of individual photographs:
L.F. Barham page number 54 (lower); M. Biscombe 74 (lower); R.G. Bullock 90 (upper); Central Garage, Brecon 21; A.B.I. Dick 69 (upper), 70, 78 (lower); The late F.E. Ellis 71 (upper); W. Grindley 13 (upper); Gwynnedd Archives 34; Hereford City Museum 10; Herefordshire Record Office 18 (lower), 36, 37 (upper); The Revd. R. Heywood-Waddington 95 (upper and lower), 96; D. Irvine 29 (upper), 31 (upper), 47, 48, 67 (lower), 68, 74 (upper), 81 (lower); J.D. Leathley 61 (upper); G.F. Lomas 44 (upper); Malvern Public Library 45, 91; Marshall, Harris & Baldwin Ltd. 25, 37 (lower), 41, 49, 55, 56, 57 (upper and lower), 87, 88, 93, 94 (upper), 104–107, 116, 119 (lower); R. Mays 77 (lower); L.E. van Moppes 44 (lower); H.G. Pitt 43 (lower); T.A. Roberts 69 (lower); Mrs G. Romsey 18 (upper); S.F. Sapp 27 (lower); G.D. Smith 59; R. Smith 14, 51 (lower); J.E. Stanford frontispiece; W.H. Summers 60 (upper and lower), 76, 77 (upper); The Hon. J.A.H. Wallace 9, 23 (upper), 40 (inset), 65, 67 (upper), 92 (upper), 108; The Brooklands Society 30; The Humber Register 42; The Midland Automobile Club 61 (lower), 78 (upper), 79 (lower), 80 (upper and lower); The National Library of Wales 7, 27 (upper), 38, 43 (upper), 52 (lower) 53, 58 (upper and lower), 75, 84, 85, 89 (upper and lower), 101 (inset), 109, 119; Watson's Motor Works, Leominster 82, 111 (upper and lower); B.B. Whitehouse 54 (upper); E. Widgery 28; Miss A. Wilkinson 46 (upper); D. Williams 19, 22 (lower); T. Williams 12, 23 (lower); Worcestershire Record Office 15, 17, 33, 39 (upper), 46 (lower), 62 (upper and lower).
The remainder are from the author's collection.

Introduction

A less formal Armistice celebration. Somebody put in hours of work (and robbed the bathroom floor of yards of covering!) to decorate this American car for the occasion. To these youngsters drawn from the three Services and the Nursing Service, belonged the next two decades. What would they make of them?

Motor-cars and motoring as a pastime had only been in existence for approximately two decades by the time the 1918 Armistice was signed. In that short period technical advances had been prodigious, whereas in the following two decades with which this book is concerned the technical advances were far less immediately apparent; one had to look beneath the surface, so to speak, to find them. To express this in another way the motor-car of 1938 was, in its capabilities and appearance, far less different from that of 1918 than was the motor-car of 1918 from that of 1898.

To regard motoring between the wars solely in the light of technical progress is to lose sight of what is perhaps the key factor in assessing the differences that distinguish the 'twenties and 'thirties motoring scene from that prior to 1914. This key factor lies much more with the social and economic climate and environment, of which motoring in the inter-war years became an increasingly significant part, rather than in the technical progress of the cars themselves.

There was such progress, of course, for cars such as the Leyland Eight, the

Lanchester Forty, the Isotta-Fraschini Tipo 8 or the Hispano-Suiza H6B and others were splendid evidence of it. These were costly machines aiming for perfection in a market where cost was of little or no consequence. Had their designers been able to look forward to 1938 they might have seen, no doubt to their dismay, to what tiny proportions that market would by then have shrunk. Rather it was Henry Ford or William Morris whose vision was to be proved the sounder, for the one consistent theme for the ensuing twenty years was the achievement of motoring for the masses; not in the cheap and crude cyclecars but in no-nonsense, go-anywhere, easy-to-maintain, inexpensive and unpretentious cars for which they rightly saw an ever-expanding market.

For the majority of motorists of, say, 1938, the car or motorcycle was merely a means of getting from A to B; true, it may have been used purely 'for pleasure' at week-ends and holidays but it was not used for motoring's sake, for the pleasures and sensations that motoring gave. Ten years earlier the majority of cars would have been used with the pleasure of motoring as an activity, a sensation, slightly uppermost, overruling the mere idea of getting from place to place; while in 1918, if one was lucky enough to own a motor vehicle at all, the pleasure of actually motoring, the sensation, was still the prime incentive. Obviously these criteria apply only in general terms to that mythical being, 'the average motorist' – to the enthusiasts of any motoring period, as for the enthusiasts for any other pastimes, different values must be applied.

In selecting the photographs the aim has been to show motoring between the wars in as wide variety as possible but inevitably much has had to be left out. Those who were motorists in this period, particularly in the earlier years of it, may well be disappointed that the make or model they best remember isn't portrayed, an omission that may be equally regretted by those whose interest in the subject stems from reasons other than of having motored in those seemingly far-off days. But no amount of photographs can be a total substitute for first-hand experience; if one has that experience one adds one's own imagination to the picture to conjure up the thousand fleeting impressions of the time . . . one can hear the individual engine note, smell the leather upholstery, recall the squeaking brakes when one was on the way to so-and-so. If one lacks that experience then, sadly, it is rather like looking through an old album that belonged to strangers . . . one sees the pictures and can recognise objects, but the essence, the momentary re-living of times, places and sensations, is lacking and one can only wonder what it was really all about. To wonder is a valuable aid to one's sense of proportion and one doesn't need to know all the answers; to wonder is good enough.

MOTOR CYCLING

Royal motor-cyclist; Prince Albert, later King George VI, with an early ohv Douglas, *c*.1920

The years between the wars saw the zenith of the British motorcycle, but it was a period during which both the pastime itself and the machines underwent a number of subtle changes. Broadly speaking, the motorcycle appealed to the sportsman in that in sporting guise it offered a performance better than could be achieved in a car except at many times the initial cost and cost of running, whereas its appeal to the tourist was predominantly that of low initial cost and upkeep, with performance coming a long way behind in his priorities.

The one fly in the ointment was the lack of weather protection and the resultant need for specialized clothing to combat the elements. This was of little consequence to the rabid sporting enthusiast who was inclined to regard even the most spartan car owner as something of a sybarite but it was of consequence to the 'potterer' or the family man.

The motorcycle had played a prominent part in the recent war and many thousands of servicemen were familiar with the trusty Triumphs and flat-twin Douglases and other machines that had given such yeoman service. Peace brought few new designs at first but the rush to become mobile caused a rash of small makers, often mere assemblers, who turned out machines of little merit. Direct belt drive was on the way out except in the lowest-powered and cheapest machines, but chain-cum-belt drive was still commonplace, as were machines lacking either a kick-starter or even a free-engine clutch. Some riders still preferred the belt to the chain on account of its smoothness but improvements in all-chain transmission were rapid and by the mid-1920s all-chain drive was clearly in the ascendancy.

So too were well-designed countershaft gearboxes, although a number of the cheaper machines only offered two speeds at first. Four speeds were available in a few instances but the most significant development was the positive-stop foot-change introduced by Velocette in 1928, though hand-change continued in wide use until the mid-1930s or so. The majority of motorcyclists made use of acetylene lighting but the Americans had long ago shown the way to electric lighting that was entirely satisfactory for motorcycles and the more expensive British machines followed suit, though for many years this refinement cost extra.

Improving performance brought the need for better brakes and the old stirrup brake of pedal-cycle origin was a pretty useless device, and indeed, the dummy belt-rim brake was little better. As the 1920s progressed internal expanding hub brakes were more extensively used, while the change from the old narrow-section beaded-edge tyres to the wider low-pressure pattern was a significant help.

With rare exceptions most frames were rigid, only the front forks being sprung, but by the close of the 1930s rear suspension and greatly improved front fork designs were evident. The coming of the cheap and reliable small car, heralded by the remarkable Austin Seven of 1922, beguiled many away from the ranks of touring and family motorcyclists, still more noticeably when small cars were available cheaply with saloon bodies, for here at one blow was removed the greatest bugbear to the family motorcyclist. However, there were still many diehards to whom the idea of motoring in a 'fug-box' was unpalatable.

Of all road users, perhaps it was the motorcyclists who were most often technically knowledgeable, friendly, and possessed of a great sense of cameraderie. To many a young man of the period dreams were centred on a Norton, a Rudge, a Velocette or what you will (for the Land of the Rising Sun was far over the motorcycle horizon then), there were no 'Hell's Angels' connotations, and he learnt a respect for machinery, for the road and for other road users that stood him in good stead on two, three or four wheels.

No event was held in higher esteem or exerted a greater influence on sporting motorcycles than the incomparable Tourist Trophy races, held in the Isle of Man since 1907 and revived in 1920. The inter-war period saw the increase in classes eligible for these races and the introduction of the Amateur TT which later grew into the Manx Grand Prix. Before the RAC ban in 1925 there were innumerable sprint events on the public roads, sand-racing provided a popular alternative, and trials courses tended to become more and more 'off the road' in order to provide tough enough tests for men and machines. The late 'twenties saw the rise of a new sport for motorcycles, the 'dirt-track' or 'speedway' which soon attracted a very big and enthusiastic following, its star performers regarded in much the same light as today's star footballers.

In all these competitive elements, as in touring, the British motorcycle still held supreme, though in the late 'thirties opposition from Continental makers was very real and to the thoughtful must have given some concern for the future.

A very early Cotton, that individualistic Gloucester make. This is one of the few early ones to be fitted with the Villiers two-stroke engine and the early form of front forks, *c.*1922

One was legally permitted to ride a motor-cycle at 14 in the early days and this rider looks little older! The machine seen in this frolic in the snow is a Crindley Sporting, a rare make made in small numbers at Prees, Shropshire, and for so small a concern, with an enviable sporting reputation. This one dates from c.1923

Head down and body flattened along the tank, a motor'cycle competitor extracts the maximum from his machine at a speed event, c.1922. The venue is probably Chatcombe Pitch near Cheltenham or Hipton Hill near Evesham

A Douglas combination provides the backdrop to this summer halt beside a country road. Any fine summer week-end in the inter-war years would find scenes like this repeated up and down the country, for the motorcycle combination provided the cheapest way of motoring for two if more comfort than that of a pillion-seat was wanted

Paterfamilias aboard a big-twin A.J.S. combination. Note the spare wheel and luggage platform astern of the sidecar

The Old Wyche Cutting,
Malvern, is the scene of
a hill-climb as part of the
1920 Victory Cup Trial
held on 24 April 1920.
Seen here is Bert
Bladder with his wife as
passenger in a New
Imperial combination
outfit

One of the legendary speed heroes of the time, George Dance . . . a name inextricably linked with speed and Sunbeams, is seen here with Bert Tetstall 'in the chair' at a speed event, c.1922

The rewards of success! Sunbeam rider Reg Brown poses beside the silverware; the picture almost certainly dates from late 1920 or early 1921, for the observant will spot the replica Tourist Trophy awarded him for his 3rd place in the 1920 Senior. The elegantly modelled motor-cyclist a-top the giant trophy on the left is worthy of note

Three British entrants in the International Six Days event of 1920 pose with their machines in the sun of Geneva. They are Eric Williams (A.J.S.), H. Gibson (Raleigh sidecar) and Newman (Douglas)

A typical provincial motor-cycle dealer's establishment displays its wares, including Rudge, Ariel, A.J.S., Douglas and Enfield machines . . . a happy reminder of the days when the British motor-cycle reigned supreme

Close-up of the engine department of a classic machine of the time, the side-valve Sunbeam. Note the superb finish of the frame and engine components

A group of A.J.S. Works riders pose with their big-twin combinations at Brooklands, with the test-hill in the background

Claude Temple beside one of his famous speed machines, this one sporting a big V-twin overhead camshaft Anzani engine

A.V. Ebblewhite ('Ebby'), the official starter, about to despatch Graham Walker (Rudge) on his way in a Manx Tourist Trophy race

Crash-hatted and in leathers, Manx Grand Prix rider
Tony Williams poses for the camera astride his ohv
Sunbeam

CYCLECARS & BABIES

The prototype 'Family' Morgan 4-seater arrived in
1912 but although production began on a very
limited scale in 1915, the 'Family' model was
announced as a post-war model. This is the 1919 car
in which E.B. Ware was often portrayed. Acetylene
lighting later gave way to electric, and the mounting
of the speedometer is of note in this early model

A 1920s' joke in that venerable journal *'Punch'* read: 'I can't come out yet, dear, I'm washing the baby', and illustrated the young wife attending to the ablutions of the baby car in the bath. Perhaps the Austin Seven was the first British car to occupy a place in the affections of the British public akin to that of the legendary Model-T Ford, the 'Tin Lizzie', in America. It was certainly a landmark in motoring history.

The cyclecar was much more closely related to the motorcycle and had enjoyed its first boom from about 1912. Usually powered by an air-cooled motorcycle engine, most cyclecars were crude in the extreme but achieved a modicum of performance by reason of a good power-to-weight ratio. The more sporting cyclecars offered performance allied to economy with marginally less exposure to the elements than a motorcycle, the better of them such as the G.N. and the Morgan having an appeal that caused them to survive, if not prosper, for a longer period than those whose only virtues were low initial cost and economy of operation.

Cyclecars underwent a revival in the years immediately after the 1918 Armistice, first because demand for anything that would motor was so great and secondly, because prices rose alarmingly and the cyclecar was about the cheapest available to an undemanding public. But what really killed the breed was the advent of the Austin Seven in 1922. Considered a joke at first, the 'Baby' Austin, as it soon came to be affectionately termed, was a large car in (very) miniature, even boasting miniscule four-wheel brakes whose stopping power was more technical than actual. But it was well built of first-class materials, had a water-cooled four-cylinder engine, electric lighting and shortly after its introduction electric starting as well, adequate weather protection, ample space for two adults and two children or one child and luggage, and was inexpensive in first cost and upkeep. One could say that it was the baby that changed motoring, if not overnight, then certainly within the decade. A saloon-bodied version was available from May 1926.

Austin's greatest rival, Morris, entered the baby car market in 1929 with the Morris Minor – at first with an overhead camshaft engine that was the inspiration for Cecil Kimber's M.G. Midget which itself sparked off a remarkable run of sports cars; Triumph brought out the Super Seven, surprisingly with hydraulic four-wheel brakes and, rather in a class of its own, the Jowett from Yorkshire carried remarkably commodious bodywork on its longer chassis and always relied on two cylinders until 1936, when Jowett introduced a flat-four and moved out of the 'baby' field.

A few others had tried to break into this market but within a short time their babies tended to put on power and weight and thus strictly speaking to move out of that particular field. But none enjoyed the success or the affection of the public that attended the Austin Seven, which, though refined and up-dated, did not finally go out of production until 1938. Its phenomenal success in all forms of motoring competition from trials to out-and-out racing is another story but certainly one that vindicates a remarkably inspired design. The Austin Seven, more than any other car, killed the cyclecar stone dead.

The child of today is the motorist of tomorrow. It is a sobering thought that if this proud youngster's pedal-car came on the market today it would doubtless fetch enough money to have bought him a very handsome new car when he was old enough to drive!

The Castle-Three Runabout was an attempt by a small firm to 'civilise' the cyclecar image. The design had a number of good points but the transmission caused serious setbacks which, with other difficulties, caused manufacture to stop after only some 350 had been completed. It was also unfortunate that, as a 3-wheeler, the weight of the car should have greatly exceeded the limit that would qualify it for the reduced rate of tax. Much was made of the fact that all wheels were quickly interchangeable and that a water-cooled 4-cylinder engine was used

Elderly sporting gentleman at the controls of a very sporting G.N. Godfrey and Nash, the progenitors of the G.N., were both of highly sporting dispositions and their product, which later developed into the Frazer Nash, was one of the most speedy and popular of the many cyclecars that were a feature of the early 1920s

A twin-cylinder air-cooled Rover Eight is dwarfed by the landaulette (probably a Daimler, judging by those wooden slats protecting the petrol tank) alongside it on a Scottish ferry. Even the rather minimal equipment of a typical early 'twenties small car of this sort was better than that of its nearest rival, the motor-cycle combination

Never too old to mind the baby! The Austin Seven, for all its peccadilloes, was an inspired design that did more for the cause of motoring for the masses than any car other, perhaps, than the Model-T of Henry Ford. This 1925 chummy, in pristine condition, is obviously the pride and joy of its elderly owner

Gordon England himself snugly seated in an early
version of his high-performance 'Brooklands' Austin
Sevens, appropriately enough in the paddock at
Brooklands. Sir Herbert Austin's 'Baby' was to
develop into a very potent infant indeed in the hands
of the racing specialists

Penultimate design in the development of the Austin
Seven as a racer, the neat little side-valver made its
first appearance at Shelsley Walsh on 18 May 1935,
Walter Baumer at the wheel of this one. The
following year saw the introduction of the twin-
overhead camshaft version developed by Murray
Jamieson . . . a far cry indeed from the funny little
baby of 1922

Even quite humble cars competed in club events at Brooklands, as witnessed by this Austin Seven 'top hat' saloon seen taking part in the J.C.C's High Speed Reliability Trial on 18 June 1927. The Austin is followed by a Frazer Nash and a Ceirano, and an unfortunate A.C. lies ditched beside the road

A pretty little Swallow-bodied Austin Seven.
Although little if any better in actual performance
than the standard versions, these Swallow-bodied
cars were much more attractively bodied and turned
out and had a great popular appeal

GOING FOR A SPIN

In the early years of the inter-war period the emphasis on motor touring, or just motoring, was for the most part that it was undertaken with due deliberation; one did not jump into the car and immediately rush off to one's destination, be it near or far. Why not? Well, we shall see that deliberation was in part an attitude of mind and in part enjoined upon one by the motor-car itself.

First, there was the starting procedure, a ritual indeed; if the motor did not start, then one repeated the ritual. Most cars had their individual whims over starting with which a sensible owner would soon learn to come to terms. Even when one enjoyed the luxury of a self-starter (not by any means universal in the early 1920s but soon becoming a *sine qua non*) one freed the engine first on the handle to reduce the load imposed on the starter motor and battery.

Previous page Far removed from the cyclecar image, this Silver Ghost Rolls-Royce shows motoring at the other end of the spectrum and is the embodiment of refinement. Here is a car that could cope with any occasion from the formal to the Grand Tour without causing a moment's misgiving

America's motor industry achieved mass production long before that of this country and the Chevrolet seen here is typical of the simple and rugged American touring car imports of the early 1920s. This 5-seater touring car undercut the Morris Cowley by quite a few pounds but its £22 annual tax as against £12 for the Morris and its heavier petrol consumption had to be borne in mind

But wait . . . one still should not actually be off on one's journey, for the motor must be allowed to warm up a little before being expected to travel under load . . . oils were less universally adaptable then than now. Even when one did get under way one was careful not to open the throttle excessively, especially in the indirect gears, until the motor had thoroughly warmed up. Soon one was bowling along the road at, perhaps, 20mph (still the legal limit).

Open touring cars predominated, either in four- or five-seater form or the then popular two-seater and dickey. The dickey, meant as an occasional accommodation, varied enormously in its appointments or the lack of them, and was passable in fine weather but excruciating in bad, and at all times somewhat unsociable, it being virtually impossible to communicate with those in front. But tourer or two-seater, the hood would be down more often than not, the top panel of the windscreen slightly open to reduce backdraught, and all aboard would be well wrapped up except in the warmest weather; in Britain's fickle climate one often had to consider the possibility of being cold or wet. To stop and erect the hood was to risk getting wetter than to motor on in the hope that the rain would diminish or cease altogether, and the much-vaunted 'one-man' hood might well take five minutes to erect by the time one had undone the hood cover and sundry straps and clips, persuaded it out of its folds and pulled at its joints to stretch the fabric gratefully over the screen pillars and nurse several sore fingers.

In really wet weather, of course, the hood was up and the sidecurtains too, and noise inside the car immediately increased and was added to by the innumerable scratchings, squeaks and groans and windy flappings of the large area of best double-duck that did its best to keep one dry. Luggage? Much depended on whether one was fussy as to whether the luggage was in the dry or not. An unoccupied dickey seat was an excellent stowage in the dry and indeed, was often so laden with the general impedimenta of motoring that it was well-nigh impossible to accommodate extra passengers. Alternatively, most tourers had ample space between the front and rear seats in which luggage could be placed and most commonly of all there was the luggage grid at the rear, exposed to the elements, so the luggage had either to be covered with a waterproof securely lashed down or one could have a purpose-built trunk.

The owner-driver was expected to have a reasonable mechanical know-ledge, enough, anyway, to cope with common minor breakdowns on the road, and with this in mind a tool-kit was carried on the car. All manufacturers provided one as a matter of course though its contents varied. Humbers, representative of the better-quality touring cars of the time, came with a tool-kit of over forty items but not all makers were as generous.

In the early 1920s most cars lacked four-wheel brakes; speeds on the whole were low and braking distances long. If one's car did have the new-fangled four-wheel brakes it was prudent to wear a red warning triangle on the rear of the car as advice of the car's allegedly superior stopping power to those astern. Most drivers were aware of the limitations of current braking systems and slowed on the engine and gearbox . . . always when descending steep hills . . . and contrived to use the brakes only in emergency or to bring the car to a stop, methods of driving that also helped to lessen the likelihood of 'the dreaded sideslip', a danger that had been ingrained into motorists almost from the first. Yes, motoring for the average motorist of the 1920s was full of deliberation.

Above and right   Owner and driver pose separately
with this charming cabriolet of the early 1920s.
Detachable rims were unusual at this date on cars of
other than American origin but could be obtained at
a customer's request even on a Rolls-Royce

This splendid example of an early 1920s sporting
tourer defies the writer's powers of recognition as to
make but displays an Edinburgh registration
number. The large low-mounted headlamps are
visible only by their reflections in the highly
polished aluminium bonnet

37

No mistaking the well-known 'Bullnose', though this one has a boot tied round its radiator cap and this, with the floral buttonholes of the passengers, suggests wedding festivities

A quiet spin down a country lane in summer with a *c.*1924 11.4 Humber. Many such lanes survived with a similar surface devoid of tarmac for another decade or more. The Humber was a typical good-quality medium touring car so characteristic of the period before saloons began to outdo open cars in popular favour. For inclement weather Humbers' weather equipment was better than most

A Rover of *c.*1924 demonstrates the virtues typical of its kind – roominess and adequate weather protection. Rovers were early users of sidescreens opening with the doors

Above An interesting group of cars, including an Alvis and a sporting Chenard-Walcker of typically French appearance, photographed in London at a time which strongly suggests the period of the General Strike of 1926

Left Reputed to be the only make of car to have been advertised in *The Church Times*, Leslie Hounsfield's highly unorthodox utility car, the Trojan, certainly appealed to orthodox churchmen, for it was the choice of many clerics. Its most optimistic top speed would not have alarmed the most timorous parishioner and it could withstand the most cruel ill-treatment with Christian meekness and fortitude. This example wears the pneumatic tyres that were available as an option for those who could not quite stomach the solids which were standard wear on the majority of Trojans

This view of a 1921 Humber 'Ten' which the RAC rated at 11.4hp reveals many features typical of motoring at this period. The upper panel of the screen is slightly open because this reduced the backdraught when the hood was down (which it was, more often than not), the mounting of the spare wheel precludes the use of a door on the driver's side, the dickey-seat (unsociable at the best of times) is, however, comfortably upholstered and provided with arm-rests and the panel in front of it could be raised to any desired angle to deflect the wind

Perhaps not 'The Hon. Bertie' himself as in the maker's advertisements but no doubt the driver of this splendid Alvis 12/50 Super-Sports would agree with that fictional hero that 'She's some car, believe me'

A cheerful party of youngsters photographed aboard an Anzani-engined Frazer Nash during a summer holiday. The Frazer Nash, a make that perpetuated chain transmission until the late 1930s, was a make of uncompromisingly sporting emphasis and individuality to which it was impossible to be indifferent . . . it inspired either an almost fanatical affection or an equally acute dislike. The young man at the wheel obviously subscribes to the former view!

A six-cylinder 24/90 Straker-Squire halts beneath the dappled shade of a wayside tree. This massively built and finely proportioned car owed something in its bevel-driven overhead camshaft design to earlier Mercedes practice, but was in fact the brainchild of the late Sir Roy Fedden

This very rare car, a 2-litre Arab of 1926, was purchased as a chassis and then had this simple but typically British two-seater body made for it for a cost of £60. Later it had a stylish fabric coupé body built for it and even later it acquired a body from a 30/98 Vauxhall. Only about a dozen Arabs were made but they were cars of a distinguished pedigree and of considerable potential

Photographed on a sunny day in Malvern, a Standard
and a 14/40 Vauxhall thread their way cautiously
down a steeply graded street; cautiously not because
of traffic but because the Standard at least is not
provided with four-wheel brakes, a deficiency that
the Vauxhall probably shares

Photographed in August 1928, this Bean 12hp tourer poses near Lichfield. Grown out of the Perry, the Bean was intended for production on a massive scale, but early optimistic target figures were never realised, matters grew worse and no Bean cars were made after 1929. It was thoughtful to include the chauffeur in this family-album picture

A singularly happy marriage between a quality American chassis, the Lincoln V8, and nicely proportioned and pleasingly unfussy British coachwork. The Lincoln greyhound leaps enticingly forward from the radiator cap and a padlock secures the spare wheel

A British-owned 2-litre Métallurgique of semi-sporting mien and boasting a single overhead camshaft engine sets off across the roads of France on its way to Switzerland in August 1926. This famous Belgian make was absorbed by its compatriot, Minerva, in the following year

Miss Violette Cordery had already made famous the name of Invicta the year before this picture was taken. This 3-litre example of the make may not have been as widely travelled as the Cordery car but illustrates its suitability for Continental touring very adequately

MOTORING...almost for the masses

Bespoke coachwork of the early 1920s, thought to be mounted on a 18CV Rolland-Pillain, known in England as the 20/30 model. Salmons & Sons Ltd were coachbuilders with Works at Newport Pagnell, Bucks, and even ventured into motor manufacture with a car known as the N.P. This venture was short-lived, but the firm later became well-known for their 'Tickford' bodies

Prior to about 1925 the closed car was largely reserved for formal occasions or town use, but as performance improved so that even the smallest cars could carry closed bodywork and as new techniques of mass production, copied from America, enabled closed bodywork to be produced cheaply, so fashion and our fickle climate brought the closed car to the fore. In 1925 the majority of makers turned out probably five or six times as many open cars as closed ones; ten years later the ratio was reversed. The sporting motorist clung most consistently to open sports cars but even he was being tempted away by sports saloons and sports coupés by the mid-1930s.

Early closed bodywork was tall, heavy and expensive and early mass-production closed cars were boxy, four-square and stark in their appointments. As the 1920s drew to a close there was a revulsion against this angularity of outline which at first produced a period of singularly unattractive high-waisted fabric-finished saloons in a misguided attempt to diminish the appearance of height and, less misguidedly, to reduce weight. The novel and patented Weymann system of silent fabric-covered construction was in a class of its own and often looked very handsome, particularly on a large chassis. Unfortunately it had many cheap and nasty imitators who used inferior materials and could not incorporate the salient design features without falling foul of the patents. Luckily they were short-lived (their shoddiness ensured that) and meanwhile great improvements were being made in mass-production techniques, so that by the mid-1930s saloon cars were no longer tall and angular but lower and better rounded in outline.

No sooner had the closed car overtaken the open car in popularity than with typical perversity its users wanted more sun and air; the sunshine roof became all the rage. Mechanically many changes were on the way, too. Much effort was directed towards simpler gear-changing. Armstrong-Siddeley popularised the 'self-change' pre-selector gearbox and to this Daimler added the fluid-flywheel and in 1931 Vauxhall became the first British makers to introduce synchromesh with their Cadet. Four-wheel brakes were the rule, not the exception, and hydraulic operation was on the increase. Coil ignition had virtually ousted the old magneto and gave easier starting but a greater dependence on the battery. This long-suffering component also had to cope with an increasing number of electrical items.

Two important safety features became legally obligatory. The first was the compulsory use of safety-glass windscreens, soon to spread to all glass; the second was compulsory third party insurance . . . sensible legislation in view of the ever-increasing traffic. The relaxation of the old 20mph speed limit did not mean an immediate free-for-all, for speed limits were widely imposed in built-up areas, giving rise to quantities of limit and de-restriction signs that formed only a small part of a rapidly increasing jungle of motoring 'street furniture'. The depression years had sent a host of motor manufacturers to the wall with the result that the 'thirties saw a process of rationalisation of models from those makers that still struggled to survive.

Town and countryside were beginning to have to come to terms with mass motor mobility and on the whole they were not very successful. The outbreak of war turned thoughts and energies into different channels and the problems that motoring of the 1930s raised were, perforce, shelved . . . only to rear their hydroid heads more urgently decades later.

This Rolls-Royce Silver Ghost of the early 1920s
reveals the legacy of Edwardian thinking in its tall
landaulette coachwork giving ample room for
formally dressed occupants. Even some of the
coachwork styles on the 'New Phantom' that
succeeded the Silver Ghost were very similar

Not an uncommon fate for elderly Rolls-Royces, this
example has been rebodied as a shooting-brake for
use on the Scottish estate of a wealthy family. Despite
its more humble status it is obviously very well cared
for

Left Early 1920s tall saloons were a legacy from the Edwardian era. The saloon body on this chauffeur-driven Darracq carries only one door on the near side, so that access to the front passenger's seat would involve the seat swivelling. This was a less convenient method than the more usual one of providing two doors on the near side but only one on the off side, the driver then having to enter or leave the car by way of the front passenger's door. On the other hand, the method adopted here did enable the chauffeur to enter or leave the car without disturbing the front passenger

Left The four-cylinder Austin Twenty made an admirable hire car, though this example is probably in private service. The chauffeur has the sort of homely face that so ably complemented this worthy but unexciting car Daimlers, with their quiet but smoky sleeve-valve engines, were popular with those who valued comfort and silence above performance. In all probability this example is a hire car, for the muffler and cloth cap would scarcely have passed muster in private service

The 1920s were probably the heyday of the mascot in a wide variety of forms. The example shown here was no extra 'goody' but a splendid device of the makers, Etablissement Ballot, Paris. In her left hand this unsuspectedly strong maiden carries a beautifully executed model of a Ballot engine, the flywheel of which is facing the viewer

Below This commodious fabric saloon of *c*.1928 is a 16/65 Lagonda which, unlike the better-known and more sporting 2-litre, was a six-cylinder car with pushrod overhead valves. Most Lagondas were massively constructed so the fabric body of this example does little to reduce a weight that limited performance to a maximum of 65mph or so. A well-appointed car, it shared many chassis features of the 2-litre, including very effective and easily adjusted brakes

Opposite This shot of an artillery-wheeled Morris Isis saloon might have come straight off the cover of *The Morris Owner*, house journal of that popular make. The Thames-side location and the smiling lady and gentleman all suggest that the publicity man was not far away

Practically unknown to Sassenachs, this car with a hint of Riley about it is the Little Scotsman of 1930 powered by the well-proven Meadows 4ED engine. One wonders how many of these saw the light of day, even North of the Border

Right The dawning 'Thirties saw an outbreak of straight-eights, particularly from America. By this time the better American cars were moving away from the wooden-wheeled, detachable rims image, as they were from the square and ugly sedan bodies characteristic of earlier styles. This Marmon-Roosevelt 8 carries attractive English drophead coupé bodywork that further enhances its appearance

Right One of the rarer body styles available on the Morris Ten of the mid-1930s was this model, complete with dummy 'pram-irons', for the coupé was a fixed head and not the costlier (and draughtier) soft-top that the 'pram-irons' were intended to suggest. Although it was but a humble Morris, ownership of this model doubtless imbued its owner with the notion that he was one up on the Jones's next door!

By the time of this shot, 1933, the General Motors influence at Vauxhall's Luton plant was complete. The Light Six seen here was available with 12hp or 14hp engine and caused sales to leap gratifyingly upward

Left It doesn't look brand-new, but they're very proud of this 1937 Standard Flying 12 saloon nevertheless. If they managed to hang on to it until after the war it would doubtless have sold for much more than the original purchase price

An old-established make, Riley picked a winner in the Nine, introduced for 1927. This 1934 Imp was one of their most attractive sports cars and was offered when the Riley Nine was at the height of a successful racing career

Two examples of the coachbuilders' art on quality chassis, a Minerva and an Invicta. The former was a wedding-present from groom to his bride and the Invicta too belonged to the same family of discerning motorists

Below Speed, comfort, looks and luxury summed up in this fine 6½-litre Bentley with Park Ward fixed-head coupé bodywork. In the days before modern ventilation systems the openable screen was a boon in hot weather and even more so in thick fog

The acme of the mid-1930s Teutonic image, this fine Horch coupé suggests power and speed in every line. Aptly, for its owner is Hans Stück von Villiez, racing motorist and hill-climb champion, who is seen talking to the Secretary of the Midland Automobile Club after that Club's Shelsley Walsh meeting of June 1936

Despite a growing popularity the motor-towed caravan was about in far fewer numbers than is the case today, and present-day caravaners would be aghast at the lack of amenities that a small 'van such as the one portrayed here had to offer . . . little more than somewhere dry in which to eat or sleep in somewhat cramped conditions. The car is a brand-new 1922 Humber 11.4, and as this family changed their car at frequent intervals it dates the picture fairly accurately

Even in the mid-1920s small cars could cope adequately with a light caravan. The cars portrayed here are a Hillman Eleven and a Humber 8/18, both of 1924. The Hillman towed the 'van and the Humber acted as tender car. This family were ardent motoring campers and regularly went far afield like this

More ambitious and roomy was this Ford-T with
Baico extension on which the caravan body was built.
This outfit was regularly used for many years by a
Herefordshire family for holidays and fishing trips.
The frilly curtains were surely a feminine touch!

Part of the crowd of sightseers and motorists and their cars who gathered to see the King and the Royal Family attend Crathie church, near Balmoral, on 20 September 1936

SPORT

When peace returned keen amateurs could obtain a
fast car relatively cheaply by using outmoded pre-
war racing cars. All three of the Humbers raced in
the 1914 T.T. appeared in post-war competition. Here
W.G. Barlow, who later raced an Aston-Martin and a
Bentley, poses in the ex-Tuck Humber of 1914. Barlow
first raced this car at Brooklands at the August Bank
Holiday Meeting, 1920

Schoolboys, as any schoolmaster knows, are inveterate scribblers and doodlers. Yes, and a high proportion of schoolboy doodles since the coming of the mechanical age have been of things mechanical, motorcars included . . . schoolboy dreams of motor-cars, the Smith Super Speedster, super-charged, of course, sleek, slim and super-fast, the sportsman's ideal, skidding perilously round this or that course . . . Brooklands, Le Mans, Monza, Montlhéry . . . and consigned by schoolmasterly hands to the wastepaper basket in exchange for two hundred lines! Sports cars have been defined in as many ways as hordes of Smith Minors have dreamed them up in the backs of old exercise books and it would be a rash man who attempted to define the sports car to suit all tastes.

The popular conception of the 1920s sports car was a rushing, roaring, skimpily-bodied machine totally devoid of comfort or weather protection and boasting an external exhaust pipe of enormous bore and cacophonous bark; that of the 1930s as a long, low, lengthily-bonneted machine with minimal ground clearance and bedewed with flashy chromium 'goodies' and at least two bonnet straps. Alas for such conceptions . . . they are merely extensions of our schoolboy dreams and deserve the same fate.

Sport is a compound of competition and enjoyment and the photographs in this section reveal how diverse was the type of car that took part. In the earlier part of the inter-war period events of all kinds were numerous. Brooklands re-opened in April 1920 and continued until the outbreak of war in 1939. As had been the case prior to 1914, speed events and hill-climbs could legally be held on the public roads (given a little co-operation from the local police); seaside resorts ran races on the promenade or on the sand, as at Skegness, Southport or Porthcawl. But spectators were often so foolhardy that, as speeds increased, much anxiety was felt and in some districts police compliance could not be obtained. The whole matter came to a head at Kop Hill in Bucks in 1925 when a serious accident befell an unfortunate spectator and the RAC imposed a total ban on such events on public roads.

This shifted the emphasis to those venues, and few there were, where such events could be held on private ground unaffected by the ban. The longest established sprint hill-climb of all, Shelsley Walsh in Worcestershire, famed before the RAC's ban, subsequently gained international status as virtually the only hill-climb venue of any real reputation in Britain. Also there was an increasing interest in road trials of the tougher, 'off-the-road' kind. Lacking, however, was any suitable road circuit for Grand Prix racing or for sports car events such as the classic Le Mans as held on the Continent. True, circuits existed in Ireland, and in the Isle of Man the 'round the town' Mannin Moar and Mannin Beg races in Douglas were the nearest equivalent to the famed Monaco Grand Prix. It was not until 1933 that England had a real road circuit with the opening of Donington Park for motor racing (motorcycle racing had been staged there as from 1931).

The photographs occasionally portray the famous but most of them intentionally portray instead some of those thousands of men, and women too, whose names never made the headlines except, perhaps, in their local papers, but without whom the Sport as it was could never have flourished.

The Hampton was a make that settled to production at Stroud, Gloucestershire, after earlier vicissitudes, where, among other things, it became associated with successful climbs of the notorious Nailsworth Ladder nearby. Normally of few sporting pretensions as a make, this example was specially tuned and bodied for use by B.S. Marshall at Brooklands where it lapped at well over 80mph in 1922

The Junior Car Club held what were termed High Speed Reliability Trials at Brooklands when members could enjoy themselves in a variety of cars in an event which took in some of the communicating roads within the circuit. In this view, taken on 18 June 1927, Bagshawe's Frazer Nash, which won the event, leads a Ceirano and a very humdrum-looking Austin Seven

It is 4.45pm on Saturday 7 August 1926 at Brooklands on the occasion of the first British Grand Prix, and one of the victorious (and overheated) Delages is seen (just) negotiating the artificial sand-barrier chicanes, with an hour and a quarter's racing and roasting still to endure. The footbridge linking the Paddock with the public enclosure carries an appropriate Delage advertisement

A bevy of officials led by Sir 'Algy' Guinness accompanied by Lionel Martin gathers round the Riley driven by C. Paul and J. Phillip during the 500-Miles Race, 24 September 1932. Sir Algernon Guinness was the RAC's Chief Steward at the time

The E.R.A. was developed by Peter Berthon, Humphrey Cook and Raymond Mays and inspired and enlivened the British racing scene in the 1930s in road and track races and also, particularly in Mays' hands, at Shelsley Walsh. Here Prince von Leiningen, an early member of the E.R.A. racing team, leads veteran E.R. Hall's M.G. Magnette away through the Fork chicane during the British Empire Trophy Race at Brooklands on 6 July 1935

A magnificent shot of Miss May Cunliffe in the 1924 2-litre Grand Prix Sunbeam, 'equipped' and taxed for the road, be it noted! Miss Cunliffe drove Bentleys and this Sunbeam with considerable success, verve and skill at Shelsley Walsh and at Southport. Beside the car stands Bill Perkins, Sunbeam's chief racing mechanic

Blackpool Promenade is the scene for this speed contest in which the competitors were sent off in pairs. Here that legendary racing Aston-Martin 'Bunny' is slightly quicker off the mark than N.T. Beardsell's racing Hodgson. A delectable Hispano-Suiza hides between the tram and the hut, and the upper-deck passengers in the tram enjoy a grandstand view

Long-distance road trials needed considerable organisation, including the use of many 'official cars' to enable officials and marshalls to cover the route. Arrayed here are five official cars and their crews for the A.C.U. Stock Trial of 1925. From left to right they are: I.D. Fell (Riley), The Revd E.P. Greenhill of the A.C.U. (Palladium), R. Abbott (Clyno), Major A.H. Loughborough of the R.A.C. (Bentley) and Richard Lisle (Star). Ray Abbott added a footnote on the reverse of the photo that 'every car was capable of over 60mph on the road'

Two competitors in the 1925 £1000 Trial tackle
Kirkstone Pass. They are T.A.N. Leadbetter's Alvis
and A.R. Abbott's Clyno. Successes gained by any
particular make in such trials were widely advertised
by the manufacturers and were a valuable aid to
sales promotion. In later years, as the trials
themselves and the cars that entered for them
became more specialised the public as a whole
became less influenced by such performances

A brace of Vauxhall 30/98s and a sporting 3-litre
Invicta halt at a checkpoint during the
London–Edinburgh Trial of 1928. This was a long-
distance classic that retained its popularity for many
years

Cornishman W.P. Uglow, a well-known trials expert
of the 1930s, takes his March Special Hillman Aero-
Minx up Doverhay in a M.C.C. Trial of the time

M.G. Midgets enjoyed many competition successes
from the time of their introduction, in road, track and
trials events. This P-type Midget carries twin
'knobbly'-tyred spare wheels and displays the fruits
of its labours proudly on the bonnet

Both Oxford and Cambridge Universities sported active motoring clubs in which keen undergraduates made up for the restrictions on motoring activities imposed by the University authorities. Here, at the C.U.A.C.'s One-Day event of the 1921 season a Sports Morris Cowley and a Rhode line up for the fun

The two University Clubs were keen rivals, never more so perhaps than in the carefree days prior to 1925 when speed trials were legal on the public roads. Here, in 1924, a Cambridge man, R.F. Summers, leaves the line at Aston Clinton, near Aylesbury, to gain fastest time of the day with his Vauxhall 30/98 in 36.9 secs.

At the many speed events going on almost every week-end in 'the season' the atmosphere was friendly and, until the disaster at Kop Hill early in 1925, restrictions were few. Already a name to reckon with in the early 1920s, Raymond Mays was to become one of the aces of speed hill-climbs. He is seen here with his famous Bugatti 'Cordon Rouge' at Madresfield in 1922

Swansong for a dying make. E.R. Hall, veteran of
many Shelsleys, takes the 2,362cc Cozette-
supercharged Arrol-Aster up the hill in September
1929. Unlikely entries of these cars in the Ulster
Tourist Trophy (the race number 61 still visible on
the body side in this shot) and the Alpine Trial
brought some publicity, but this was the last fling for
the unforunate marriage between Scotland and
Wembley that united Arrol-Johnston with Aster, the
firm going into liquidation in that same year, 1929

Being on private ground Shelsley Walsh was
unaffected by the 1925 ban and gained immeasurably
in popularity and stature, achieving international
status by 1930. In 1931 Spain sent two Nacional
Pescaras to the hill, driven by Zanelli and Tort. They
failed either to take f.t.d. or the record and this view
shows Zanelli's car at the top of the hill. On the left is
Earl Howe's ex-Caracciola Mercedes-Benz

Below Malcolm Campbell was a household name between the wars and here, eagerly watched as usual, he comes up to the start line at Shelsley Walsh in his sleek Sunbeam in May 1935, but Mays' 39.6 seconds won the day and the record

Historic moment! Raymond Mays about to make the first under-40 seconds climb of Shelsley Walsh with his E.R.A. in May 1935. Expectancy is written clear on every face and they were not to be disappointed

Shelsley Walsh engendered a whole tribe of
'Shelsley Specials', often amateur-built but all
inspired by the one idea of getting up the hill as fast
as possible. As in this example many of them
dispensed power and noise in unashamed
nakedness; this is the 'Joystick Special' seen about to
go into action at the September 1935 event

A.F.P. Fane brings his
Frazer Nash-BMW
through the Esses at
Shelsley Walsh watched
by a dense crowd at the
June 1936 meeting.
These cars offered a new
concept of sports car
motoring that was only to
be fully developed after
the second world war

An all-female crew this time for the Monte Carlo Rally of 1933. This Hillman 'Wizard' was driven from John O'Groats by Barbara Marshall, Agnes Gripper and Katherine Martin, all experienced competition drivers. They had many minor adventures en route, including an involuntary fire, but reached Monte Carlo successfully and were awarded the Ladies Cup for the John O'Groats entrants

The Hon. Mrs Victor Bruce at the wheel of a Hillman Straight-8 'Segrave' sports saloon in which she entered for a Monte Carlo Rally, starting from Lapland. Her husband had been the first Britisher in a British car, an A.C., to win the event some years earlier

Land speed record holders were ever popular
heroes and every schoolboy could recite the exploits
of Sir Malcolm Campbell and his 'Bluebirds'. Hidden
beneath this ingenious mock-up is a very prosaic
Citroen. The date is probably between February
1931 and February 1932, but even so somebody got
their sums wrong, Campbell's speeds on both
occasions differing from the legend on the tail

SERVING THE PUBLIC

One of the most successful of steam wagon makers
was Sentinel of Shrewsbury, and this is one of their
models. Many steam operators perpetuated the
tradition of elaborate painting and lining out; the
livery of this example was bright scarlet with black
chassis and running gear, and the gold lettering was
elaborately shaded. This wagon carries its fleet
number, 16. Most of the fleet were also steamers

Almost from the earliest days of the motor age the motor vehicle, with substantial assistance from the steam vehicle for heavy work, was pressed into the service of the public, and never was its worth better vindicated than in the 1914–18 war. The developments of the inter-war years were significant and far-reaching, primarily in the fact that for the first time road transport in the service of the public became a serious challenge to the long-held supremacy of the railways instead of being ancillary to them.

Improved techniques of tyre construction enabled heavy vehicles to use pneumatics instead of the solids hitherto almost universal, a development first favoured for passenger vehicles and later spreading to goods vehicles as well. The introduction and spread of the diesel-engined vehicle and discriminatory tax legislation forced the steamer, popular for the heaviest jobs, off the roads, and the articulated lorry, introduced in six-wheeler form to Britain by Scammell in 1920, led the way to higher payloads.

During the 1920s small country bus services proliferated, many of them started by ex-service men with war-time vehicles adapted for the job and later with purpose-built vehicles, and what a valuable, personal and friendly service they performed, buses and staff known and often nicknamed by all, accommodating and adaptive as no urban bus service could ever be. Even the railways themselves ran feeder services, seemingly unaware of the threat to their own existence that they posed.

Steam had by no means lost the battle for the really heavy jobs until forced out by partisan legislation and the spreading use of the diesel lorry in the 1930s. These three are the products of Mann's Patent Steam Cart & Wagon Co, of Leeds, and show every sign of leading a hard life

Right It's new, it's theirs and they're proud of it. The Model-T Ford, 'Tin Lizzie' of popular concept, was a widely-used and long-suffering vehicle that could still be found as a willing worker at a ripe old age. Even the signwriter has enjoyed himself

Charabancs, high, unwieldy and crammed with usually noisy pleasure-seekers, or empty and simmering in the afternoon seaside sun awaiting a mystery tour, were popular in holiday areas, but by the late 'twenties had largely given place to more sophisticated long-distance coaches which offered cheaper fares than the railways. In smaller vehicles and for shorter journeys the variety was as great as the purposes to which the vehicles were put, even the battery-electric surviving in urban areas for the whole of the period under review, while for specific purposes such as house-to-house milk delivery their use increased.

As for the hire car or taxi (London's taxis being creatures apart), almost every village could boast at least one by the 1930s and what a splendidly varied assortment of ageing automobiles most of them were, ranging from the humdrum to the faded gentility of former exotica eking out their days in frowsty but dignified shabbiness.

A line-up of Bryant & May's lorries that reminds us of the days when most heavies were on solids (only one of the group is pneumatically shod) and when a transport fleet was immaculately maintained – just look under those bonnets – and drivers were expected to wear uniform

The pen is mightier than the sword! An ex-RFC Crossley converted to a publicity vehicle in the form of a letter-box . . . on the assumption, of course, that the letters would all be written with 'the' pen. The outfit manages to convey a covertly sporting impression, nevertheless

Uniformed driver, white-coated assistant. Note the ladder at the back to give access to the tea-chests carried up aloft, and the fleet number – 945 – which gives some idea of the Company's business

A war-time Continental-engined Morris Cowley fitted with a new commercial traveller's body which seems designed only to carry a coffin! Perhaps small samples would be a more likely explanation. The registration number is an Oxford one of pre-1921

Wireless was all the rage when this 'bullnose' Morris advertised its owner's wares. One can just imagine the magic sounds of 2LO emerging from that vast loudspeaker but it must have swallowed some miles per hour in drag

A Fiat and two Sunbeams in use as hire cars pose with their drivers, 1925. Not all hire cars were maintained so immaculately, but to keep them so must have been an excellent advertisement for Mr Rayner's business

'Stand for Licensed Taxis Only' proclaims the notice, and its guardian has certainly been a licensed taxi for very many years. Such Edwardian relics could be found plying for hire well into the 1930s, their engines becoming wheezier and their upholstery mustier as the years went by

Fire engines have always had a glamour of their own and this Morris-Commercial engine, newly delivered to Upton-on-Severn, has brought the local dignitaries out to welcome it

Did the sun shine more often in the 1920s than now, or was it just that photographers shunned wet days? A Lancia bus seeks the shade beside a Morris two-seater, while on the sunny side of the street a small charabanc conceals its occupants behind a voluminous hood and a Daimler landaulette awaits a hiring

This J-type Thornycroft chassis carries a splendid charabanc body with a nautical theme of positively Gilbertian extravagance and termed the Land Yacht 'Viking'. Note the nautical air given to the details of the rubbing-strake, the door and grab-handles, even to a jackstaff. If your leanings to a life on the ocean wave restricted your activities to those of a landlubber, this was just the tour for you, and when it was over you could retire to the bar, splice the mainbrace and relive it all over again

5143·3

Left A rather later Thornycroft charabanc of decidedly purposeful appearance . . . waiting to be christened 'Dreadnought' perhaps? The difficulties of folding or erecting that hood may well be imagined!

The Thornycroft A-series were popular, particularly with small operators in country districts. One is reminded of how one really had to climb up into early buses, the high chassis and body line necessitating the guard rails beneath the body sides. This one was supplied to the Isle of Thanet Electric Supply Co

Left, below A Daimler bus of about 1921. Passenger vehicles were quicker to turn to the advantage of pneumatic tyres than were goods vehicles, but this example still wears solids, the distinctive rumble of which is now a forgotten sound

The lower body line, the pneumatic tyres and the forward control all emphasise the progress made since the days of the Daimler (*See* p.94). Roads have progressed too; what is seen in the background here typifies the mid to late-1930s

This Leyland Titan, again in Southdown service, shows more modern styling and also tells of war again, not only by the white circle on the rear panel as an aid in the blackout but by the producer gas unit in use as a fuel economy measure

REPAIRS & REPLENISHMENTS

Suburban motorist's Saturday morning chore . . . it
wouldn't be 'done' to clean the car on Sunday then
. . . in readiness for the family outing. This shot
reminds one of how tall one's garage needed to be
even for an average-sized family car in the 1920s.
Note also the four-wheel brake warning triangle and
the rails protecting the rear panel from any luggage
on the grid, seen in its folded position

Cars breed garages, garages breed cars . . . a chicken-and-egg situation perhaps. A noteworthy feature of the inter-war period was not simply the increase in numbers of cars and garages which was only to be expected, but a changing relationship between the two as compared with the earlier years of motoring. Prior to 1914 garages, large or small, were almost invariably part and parcel of a settlement . . . town or city or even village. In the next two decades a change became increasingly apparent, caused by two entirely separate developments. The first was the adoption of the petrol pump in place of the hitherto universal can; the second was the building of arterial roads expressly for motor traffic rather than Chesterton's 'rolling English road' of earlier times. The motor-car's own contribution was the mobility it gave.

These new factors gave rise to the filling-station, made possible by the petrol pumps and required at intervals along the lengthy new arterial roads even well away from existing settlement, and reached by the operator by motor as easily as by his customers. It was not a garage in the strict sense; it dispensed fuel and lubricating oils essentially, and often tyres and accessories as well. It did not buy, sell or repair cars, though in many cases it sold sweets, cigarettes and sundries. It did its job with varying efficiency but too often it became an eyesore, smothered with garish advertisements, untidy, a ready depository for the motorists' litter and the owners' mechanical junk.

Sometimes it blossomed, if that is the word, into that other phenomenon of the time, the roadhouse . . . forerunner of the motel, a product of a pleasure-seeking age that largely relied on the motor for its pleasures, and all too often as brash and tasteless in its conception and execution as in its service to its customers. However, it apparently fulfilled their needs.

Unfortunately the public service sector was often no less an offender in the part it played in the spoiling of the countryside. The architectural standards of the best of Victorian railway stations were not those of the bus and coach operators . . . bus and coach stations tended to be utilitarian eyesores, all too frequently tucked away (perhaps mercifully) behind ugly backs of existing buildings, or wide open spaces like overgrown car-parks, draughty, exposed to the elements and a paradise for litter.

Those with an eye for the ephemera of motoring will
find much to satisfy them in the early signs and the
Pratts' petrol pump at the kerbside. The nearer of the
two cars is an early Tipo 501 Fiat, one of the most
popular of that company's offerings

Mass-production (copied from America) made cheap transport more widely available but planted the seeds of traffic jams and overcrowding. The coming of the petrol pump brought a mushroom growth of filling-stations; this newly-opened premises dispensed R.O.P. . . . Russian Oil Products

Right A delivery of Overland cars and a light van, together with a solitary 14hp Crossley tourer (fifth from left) to a small town garage, *c.*1924. American cars were popular in outlying districts on account of their lack of complication and relatively powerful but 'woolly' engines. The standard sedan (far left) contrasts strongly with the English-bodied landaulette next to it

Many such filling-stations rapidly became disfigured
by a rash of indiscriminate advertisements and signs,
adding what might be termed an unsightly chapter to
motoring architecture. This example is less untidy
than many

Quality secondhand cars in the showrooms of
Watkins & Doncaster Ltd, of 95A Great Portland
Street, London, c.1922. The lettering on the windows
proclaims the firm to be agents for Daimler,
Wolseley, Talbot, Sizaire-Berwick, Swift, Enfield-
Alldays, Farman, Lanchester, Sunbeam, and Siddeley
cars . . . now almost all forgotten names

Morris, Austin, Standard, Citroen and Rover cars are
clearly visible in this mid-1920s view of the
secondhand department of a large provincial garage.
The ratio of only one saloon to seven tourers or
coupés is typical but was soon to change in favour of
the closed car

Perhaps this was rather a special sales week!
Anyway, there are the potted palms in the best
Olympia tradition and a large array of family cars,
including examples of Austin, Standard, Swift and
Singer. By now, the early 1930s, saloons predominate
even on a small chassis

A view of Clement Talbot Ltd's Barlby Road bodyshop, *c.*1934. It reveals a mass of interesting detail relevant to the better quality production, as distinct from bespoke, coachbuilding still largely using traditional methods

H. SYKES & SONS, Milton Street, Peterborough.   Tel. 2444.
We Buy and Sell Cars, Lorries, Aircraft, &c.
Second-hand Spares for any kind of Vehicle.
Welding, Cutting and Metal Salvaging Depot.

The aircraft add a touch of the unusual and the motor
vehicles would warm the cockles of the present-day
collectors' hearts. Scenes like this are a reminder
that in the depression years many a large car was
driven into a scrapyard in near-perfect condition and
that in those seemingly far-off days one could
purchase a 'runner' for almost literally a bob or two

TRAFFIC & ACCIDENTS

Daimler in distress! This solid-tyred Daimler bus appears to have suffered little damage in its encounter with the parapet but it's just as well it stopped where it did; whoever scrambled out of the open door probably did so very gingerly

The restrictions of 1914–1918 naturally reduced greatly the number of motor vehicles in use in Britain and in fact it was not until 1920 that the number of private cars and the number of motor vehicles of all sorts exceeded the previous highest total. By the census of 1925 the total of all motor vehicles in Britain topped the million mark for the first time, out of which total private cars accounted for 695,634. By 1931, however, the total of private cars alone had exceeded the million mark with a figure of 1,103,715 according to figures published by The Society of Motor Manufacturers and Traders. In the same year, 1931, that body also published figures of accidents attributed to road vehicles of all kinds, and for all classes of road vehicles the number of fatal accidents was said to be 5,746 and non-fatal accidents 129,756 for the year. Out of these totals, private cars were said to have contributed 1,813 and 48,307 respectively . . . figures which, in the light of the many fewer vehicles then than today and of the lower average speeds of the time, are grisly reminders of the toll of death and injury that an increasing subservience to the motor vehicle brought with it.

These figures do throw into perspective the widely believed and nostalgic notion that in the inter-war period the roads were blissfully open and free, just as they highlight the salient difference between motoring, in general terms, in the 'twenties and 'thirties as compared with the pre-1914 era. The inter-war years made plain the need for increasing control over the ever-increasing volume of traffic. It was not until the late 'twenties that roads designed, not adapted, as motor roads came into being, something that gained momentum until 1939. The majority of roads were still, of course, those that had served the pre-motor age, modified only in respect of surface and detail; such roads still form the greater part of Britain's road mileage even today, their inadequacy ever more apparent.

Whether or not the motor car is worth the enormous cost both in financial and environmental terms that we see today is outside the scope of these remarks; the fact remains that the new arterial roads and by-passes of the 'thirties were mostly far uglier than today's motorways, and it was in those same years that the increasing volume of motor traffic began to be a real threat to many aspects of the social environment.

One looks at the photographs of the period and reads into them only too readily an impression of uncrowded and unfettered spaciousness (in traffic terms) compared with what we know today; the figures quoted show the other side of the coin.

Before and after! This Riley Redwing has suffered a nasty thump on the nose, but in the days before unitary construction only the worst crunches were incapable of repair and skilled labour was plentiful and cheap. A pity not to have awaited the screen and spare tyre before photographing their handiwork

Much less fortunate was this 'bullnose' Morris
brought in on the good old towing ambulance that
one still occasionally sees rusting and abandoned in
country garages. The dire effects of broken
windscreens in the days before safety-glass became
compulsory can be seen in this picture and give
point to the frequent advertisements in the press of
the time advocating its use

Main street in a county town in the late 1920s;
although the tracks of the former tramway system are
still evident, the trams themselves have been
withdrawn, thus easing the congestion inevitable
previously, and within a year or so the tracks too will
have vanished

Only in recent times have conservationists revolted against the mass of ugly street furniture that mass-motoring brought with it and which did so much to mar our townscapes. Here is a reminder . . . a street without these disfigurements and without even a prowling traffic warden. Examples of Alvis, Austin, Jowett, Morris, Standard and Vauxhall cars may be seen

BROAD STREET, LUDLOW.

The air of spaciousness and lack of congestion in each of these two views of provincial towns in the 1932–38 period is accentuated by the lack of road markings or signs; parking is easy and free and there is no obstruction to moving traffic. How much the motorist of today has lost!

Burford.

220934.J.V. BRIDGE STREET AND POST OFFICE, ANDOVER

Traffic held up in Parliament Square, London, in the summer of 1932. The splendid 3-litre Bentley (then by no means a new car) in the foreground seems slightly aloof and straining for the open road . . . could this be Lord Peter Wimsey off to a case?

Traffic en route to the Derby passes through Ewell West on Derby Day, 1931. The procession reveals a splendid variety of vehicles

Traffic to the seaside, early 1930s. Nose-to-tail is no modern phenomenon, as this line of traffic approaching Aberystwyth shows. Examples of Hillman Minx, 'flat-rad' Morris and Rover may be seen among the private cars and a Maudslay bus wearing oil sidelamps and a Morris-Commercial head inland. Many of the bystanders appear awed by the volume of traffic . . . perhaps they're all waiting to cross the road, Hore-Belisha's famous beacons not yet having arrived on the scene

A Hillman Minx used by Thornycroft's mobile staff exhibits war-time lighting restrictions and the white paint to aid visibility in the blackout. Look under the bonnet, so to speak, and there you will find petrol rationing, low-octane 'Pool' petrol and all the limitations and restrictions of motoring in war